Painting Faces

Rebecca Siddiqui
Photographs by Lindsay Edwards

Contents

Goal

To paint a tiger face and a butterfly face

Materials

You will need:

• paint for the tiger face

- paint for the butterfly face

- brushes

- a big card for the boy's face

- a big card for the girl's face

Steps

The Tiger Face

1. Put yellow paint on the boy's face.

Let the paint dry.

2. Put white paint
around his eyes
and around his mouth.

3. Put black paint

on his nose.

4. Paint a small black line
   from his nose
   down to his mouth.

5. Paint long black **eyebrows** down to his nose.

6. Paint black stripes on his face.

7. Paint **whiskers**

on his cheeks.

Steps

The Butterfly Face

1. Put yellow paint on the girl's face.

   Let the paint dry.

2. Paint blue wings around her eyes.

3. Paint blue wings

on her cheeks.

4. Paint big green dots

on the wings

on her cheeks.

5. Paint little lines
down the girl's nose.

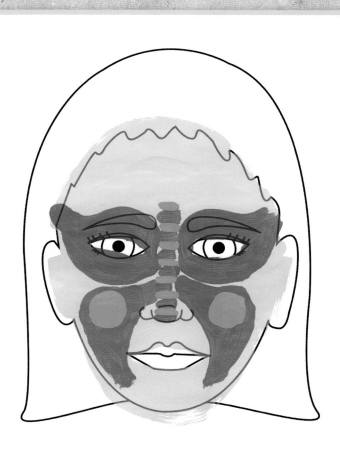

6. Paint two red lines
to look like **antennae**.

7. Paint red dots

on the antennae.

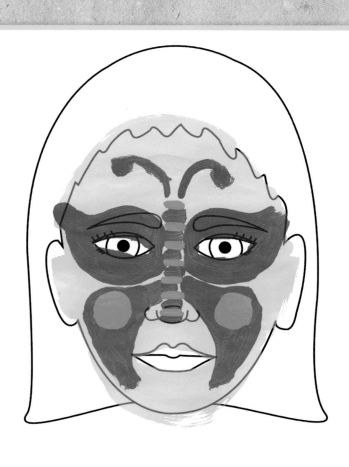

Glossary

antennae

eyebrows

whiskers